Mountain Makin's
in the Smokies

a cookbook

Published by
Great Smoky Mountains Association
1957

© 1957, © 2004 by Great Smoky Mountains Association

EDITED BY: Mary Ruth Chiles and Mrs. William P. Trotter
ILLUSTRATED BY: Mrs. Patsy Gilbert
COMPILED BY: The wives of park service employees and their friends
COVER PHOTOGRAPHS: Tom Grey and National Park Service, Great Smoky
      Mountains National Park

Printed in the United States of America

♲ This book was printed on Hopper Proterra paper which contains
60% recycled fibers, including 30% from post-consumer sources. Great
Smoky Mountains Association advocates the efficient use of recycled
and recyclable materials in its publications.

     5 6 7 8 9 10

ISBN 0-937207-12-8

WARNING: Do not eat any wild food without first positively identifying
the plant. The authors and publisher of this book assume no liability for
injuries which may occur to readers of this book who prepare foods
described in this book.

GREAT SMOKY MOUNTAINS
ASSOCIATION

Great Smoky Mountains Association is a private, nonprofit organization
which supports the educational, scientific, and historical programs of
Great Smoky Mountains National Park. Our publications are an
educational service intended to enhance the public's understanding and
enjoyment of the national park. If you would like to know more about
our publications, memberships, guided hikes and other projects, please
contact:

Great Smoky Mountains Association
115 Park Headquarters Road
Gatlinburg, TN 37738
(865) 436-7318   www.SmokiesStore.org

Great Smoky Mountains Association
Gatlinburg, Tennessee 37738

PREFACE

The early settlers in the Great Smokies were, of necessity, a self-sufficient folk. Isolated as they were, they had to grow their own food. Those were the days before supermarkets. Cornmeal was a staple item. Molasses was used in cooking and honey for table "sweet'nin'." Each little farm had its own corn field, its sorghum patch, and its bee "gums." Somewhere along the creek was a small mill where corn was ground into cornmeal.

In this booklet we have brought together some of the "old-timey," as well as some of the present-day, ways of using these staples: cornmeal, molasses, and honey. In addition, a few other recipes are included. All recipes have been used by the donors; many have been handed down from grandmother to mother to daughter.

It is the hope of the editors that you try these recipes and have fun — and good eating — while doing so.

ASH CAKE

There is an old man that lives near us that says his mother makes ash cakes all the time.

2 cups cornmeal
1 cup buttermilk
¾ teaspoon soda
⅓ cup fat
1 teaspoon salt
Enough water to make a thick dough

Have a good hot fire. Pull out ashes and make a nest-like place in the ashes. Brush off ashes down to the hearth. Put your dough in nest. Let set a while and the dough will form a crust. Then cover with ashes and hot embers. Bake 20 or 30 minutes.

Mrs. Ben C. Fisher

CORN BREAD

2 cups cornmeal
¼ teaspoon soda
2 teaspoons baking powder
1 teaspoon salt
2 eggs, beaten
2 cups sour milk
2 tablespoons melted fat

Sift together dry ingredients. Add eggs to milk and stir into dry ingredients. Add melted fat. Pour into a hot greased pan about 8 inches square, and bake at 425°, 20 to 30 minutes. Makes 6 servings.

Mrs. Guy Cable

HINT

For the best cornbread you should use an iron skillet, and the skillet should be hot before putting in the batter. The bread should be cooked in a hot oven, 475-500°. The quicker you cook it, the better it is.

EGG CORN BREAD

Chop a quarter of a pound of butter with one quart of cornmeal (white). Add a heaping teaspoon of salt, and the yolks of 4 eggs. Stir in gradually a quart of cold milk. Beat until it forms a smooth batter. Butter the pan in which the bread is to be baked. Beat the whites of 4 eggs to a stiff froth, stir them into the batter lightly and quickly. Pour into a buttered pan and bake in a moderate oven 30 minutes or until a broom-straw run into the thickest part of the loaf can be withdrawn clean.

Mrs. J. O. Morrell

INDIAN BEAN BREAD

4 cups cornmeal
2 cups cooked colored beans
½ teaspoon soda
2 cups boiling water

Put cornmeal into bowl, mix in beans that have been drained. Hollow out in meal a place to put soda and water. Make a dough stiff enough to form balls. Drop balls into a pot of boiling water. Cook about 45 minutes or until done. Serve with cooked greens and pork.

Mrs. Roy Pilkington

CHESTNUT BREAD

Peel one pound of chestnuts and scale to take off the inside skin. Add enough cornmeal to hold chestnuts together, mixing chestnuts and cornmeal with boiling water. Wrap in green fodder or green corn shucks, tying each bun securely with white twine. Place in a pot of boiling water and cook 2 hours. Salt when eating, if desired. Makes 5 or 6 buns. Bean Bread can be made the same way, but cook beans 30 minutes or more before adding cornmeal.

Mrs. Ben C. Fisher

The Indians taught us how to make Chestnut Bread and Bean Bread.

CORNBREAD

meal bin made from a hollow log

¾ cup cornmeal
1 cup sifted flour
1 teaspoon salt
4 teaspoons baking powder
4 tablespoons sugar
1 egg, well beaten
1 cup sweet milk
3 tablespoons shortening, melted

Mix and sift dry ingredients. Combine well beaten egg and milk and add to dry ingredients. Stir in shortening. Pour batter into two greased 8-inch layer cake pans. Bake in hot oven (375°) for about 30 minutes. Cut in pie shaped pieces. Split and spread butter between layers.

Mrs. Carlos T. Huskey

CORNBREAD

½ cup sugar
2 eggs
2 tablespoons shortening
1 cup sweet milk
½ teaspoon salt

1 cup cornmeal
1 cup flour
1 teaspoon soda
2 teaspoons baking powder

Mix all dry ingredients, milk, eggs, and melt shortening and add last. Bake at 450° for 25 to 30 minutes. This makes an 8-inch square panful or 9 servings.

Mrs. H. Wayne Norton

SALT RISING BREAD

Sponge: 1 cup milk
2 tablespoons cornmeal
1 teaspoon salt
2 tablespoons sugar

2nd Sponge: 1 cup lukewarm water
1 teaspoon salt
1 tablespoon sugar
2 tablespoons shortening
2 cups sifted flour

Dough: 2¼ cups sifted flour

Scald milk, then cool to lukewarm; add cornmeal, salt, and sugar. Pour into bowl. Cover and place in a warm place. Let stand for 6 or 7 hours, or until signs of fermentation (gas bubbles) appear. Then add ingredients of 2nd sponge. Beat thoroughly and again cover and place in a pan of hot water (120°). Let rise until very light; then add remaining flour gradually, until dough is stiff enough to be kneaded. Knead 15 to 20 minutes. Shape into two loaves. Place in greased pans. Brush tops with melted shortening. Cover and let stand until more than doubled in size. Bake in moderate oven (375°) 10 minutes, then lower heat to 350°, and bake 25 to 30 minutes.

Mrs. Dewey R. Ealy

corn grater

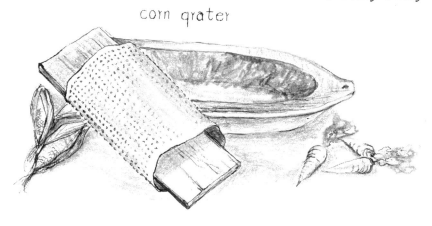

HOP YEAST using CORNMEAL

This recipe was given to me by my mother; she used it years ago. Her mother (my grandmother) made all her own yeast from hops she grew on a vine. This recipe no doubt is quite old, because my mother is almost 70 years old and my grandmother has been gone for nearly 40 years. She probably acquired it from her mother or friends.

Place hops in container, pour water over them until they are ⅔ covered. Bring to a boil, let boil 2 or 3 minutes, long enough to draw strength from the hops. Drain off liquor and while it is still hot, stir into the liquor either white or yellow cornmeal, enough to thicken. Then spread the mixture on a cloth or board and let dry.

This yeast can be used for making bread, buckwheat cakes, or wherever yeast is used.

Mrs. Stanley Cooley

OLD FASHIONED CORN LIGHT BREAD

4 cups boiling water
1 cup cornmeal

Make a mush by slowly adding meal to boiling water. Let cook about 10 minutes. Cool mush by adding 6 cups cold water. Then add enough meal to thicken. Let sour overnight in a warm place.

Then add:
½ cup sugar
½ cup molasses
1 tablespoon salt
2 tablespoons shortening

Pour into a well greased pan or skillet. Bake in a slow oven 45 to 60 minutes.

Mrs. Dewey R. Ealy

CORNMEAL LOAF BREAD

First Step: Into three cups of boiling water, put enough meal to make a stiff mush; set off stove; add 2 cups cold water and enough meal to make the consistency of cornbread. Add 1½ tablespoons salt, and let set 4 to 6 hours.

Second Step: To the above mixture add:

> ½ cup sugar
> 1 cup sorghum molasses
> 1 teaspoon soda
> 1½ teaspoons baking powder
> 1 cup flour
> 2 eggs
> ½ cup lard
> Enough meal to be like a rather
>   stiff corn bread

Cook in a greased loaf pan very slowly (250°), for 2½ to 3 hours. Before taking from oven, heat may be turned up to brown if desired.

This bread is very good with barbecued or most kinds of meat.

Mrs. W. T. Rolen

coffee mill

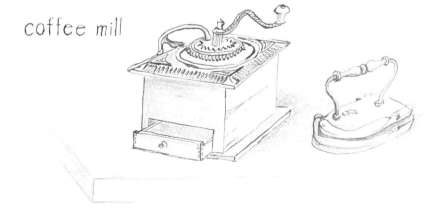

7

CORN LIGHT BREAD

1 teaspoon soda
1 teaspoon salt
¼ teaspoon baking powder
2 cups cornmeal
½ cup sugar
4 tablespoons shortening
2 cups buttermilk
½ cup flour

Put sugar, salt, soda, and baking powder in a bowl and add buttermilk. Stir well. Then add cornmeal and flour alternately. Melt shortening in a loaf pan and add to mixture. Sprinkle a little cornmeal in loaf pan. Heat pan, and pour batter into the hot pan. Bake in moderate oven (350°) 45 to 60 minutes.

Mrs. Dewey R. Ealy

CORNMEAL BISCUITS

¾ cup scalded milk
1 cup cornmeal
2 tablespoons shortening
¾ teaspoon salt
1 cup white flour
4 teaspoons baking powder

Save ¼ cup measured flour for board. Pour scalded milk over cornmeal, add shortening and salt. When cold, add sifted flour and baking powder. Roll out lightly on floured board. Cut with biscuit cutter and bake in greased pan in hot oven 15 to 20 minutes.

Mary Ruth Chiles

HUNTER'S CORNMEAL CAKE

1 cup cornmeal   ¼ cup fat
¾ teaspoon salt   Pinch of soda
Add baking powder if you have it; if not bake without
Hot water enough to make a thick dough

Have a nice clean board, oak or birch. Place dough on board and place before an open fire and bake.

My husband used to go hunting before there was a National Park, and this is how they made bread in the mountains.

Mrs. Ben C. Fisher

MILK SPILL-OVER CORN BREAD

1 egg
2 cups sweet milk
1⅓ cups cornmeal
⅓ cup flour

1 teaspoon salt
2 teaspoons baking powder
3 tablespoons bacon fat

Beat egg. Add 1 cup milk, cornmeal, flour sifted with baking powder and salt. Melt fat in large drip pan (9x13 in.); add fat to cornmeal mixture. Pour in pan. (It will be thin in pan.) Pour over the remaining 1 cup milk. Do not stir. Bake 25 minutes in 350° oven.

Mrs. Robert F. Gibbs

CRISPY CORN BREAD

6 tablespoons flour
1½ teaspoons baking powder
1 tablespoon sugar
½ teaspoon salt

¾ cup cornmeal
1 egg, beaten
½ cup milk
2 tablespoons melted shortening

Sift together flour, baking powder, sugar, and salt. Add cornmeal. Then add egg, milk, and shortening. Stir just enough to mix well. Put in well-greased pan. Bake in hot oven (425°) about 25 minutes.

Mrs. R. Leslie Chiles

CORNMEAL CAKE

1 cup cornmeal
2 cups flour
¾ to 1 cup sugar
2 tablespoons fat

2 teaspoons baking powder
½ teaspoon salt
1 egg
1 cup sweet milk

One cup of sour milk may be used in the place of sweet milk; if so use ½ teaspoon of soda with it.

Bake 25 or 30 minutes in a 375° oven.

Mrs. David C. Smelcer

CRACKLING BREAD

The skins and residue left from the renderings of pork fat at hog-killing time make cracklings. Ask a Southerner whose memory goes back far enough about crackling bread crumbled up in buttermilk — and watch his eyes light up!

2 cups cornmeal
1 teaspoon baking powder
½ teaspoon salt
⅔ cup cracklings

Sift into a bowl the cornmeal, baking powder and salt. Pour into this enough boiling water to make a stiff batter. Add cracklings. (Meat skins packaged for canapes make a passable substitute: one whole cup plus 2 tablespoon bacon drippings.) Mold into oval shapes (pones), and bake in hot (425°) oven until light brown. Serve with tall glasses of very cold buttermilk, and instructions that the hot crackling bread is to be broken up into the milk and eaten with iced teaspoons.

Mrs. Henry W. Lix

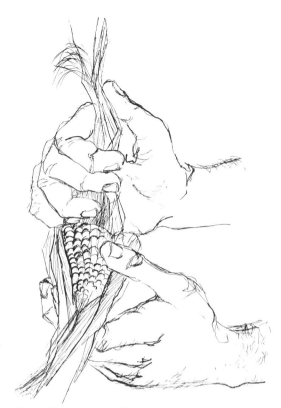

CRACKLING BREAD

3 cups cornmeal
1 teaspoon salt
3 teaspoons baking powder
1 cup sweet milk
1 cup broken cracklings

Sift dry ingredients, then add the milk and cracklings. Form into small long rolls on a baking sheet, and bake 20 minutes in a moderate oven.

Mrs. W. P. Trotter

CRACKLING BREAD

½ cup cracklings
2 cups buttermilk
3 cups cornmeal
⅓ to ½ cup water, enough to make a soft batter

1¼ teaspoons soda
1 teaspoon salt

Bake 20 or 30 minutes until good and brown.

My mother taught me how to make this bread. She was raised near the Chimneys picnic area. The last time she came to see me, in 1939, she visited the picnic area, and found the rock that they dried their wool on when she was a girl.

Mrs. Ben C. Fisher

12

SMOKY MOUNTAIN SPOON BREAD

1 cup cornmeal
½ cup flour
2 eggs
3 tablespoons melted shortening

1 cup milk
2 teaspoons baking powder
1 teaspoon salt

Sift all dry ingredients. Combine eggs, milk, and shortening. Stir until smooth. Turn into greased shallow pan and bake in hot oven (400°) for 30 minutes.

Mrs. W.P. Trotter

SPOON BREAD

1 cup cornmeal
2 cups cold water
2 teaspoons salt

1 cup milk
2 or 3 eggs
2 tablespoons fat

Mix meal, water, and salt. Boil 5 minutes, stirring. Add milk, well beaten eggs, and fat. Mix well. Pour into well greased hot pan or baking dish. Bake 50 minutes at 375°. Serve from container.

Mrs. R.P. White

SPOON BREAD

This recipe was found in Thomas Jefferson's files.

Scald 1 quart milk and ¼ teaspoon salt. Sprinkle in very slowly 1 cup cornmeal. Cook in a double boiler one hour. Add 3 tablespoons butter and 3 eggs. Mix well. Bake in oven 45 minutes.

Mrs. W.P. Trotter

BOSTON BROWN BREAD

This is my mother's old recipe for brown bread.

1 cup flour	1 teaspoon soda
1½ cups sour milk	1 teaspoon baking powder
1½ cups cornmeal	½ teaspoon salt
½ cup molasses	½ cup raisins (if desired)

Sift together dry ingredients. Mix well with sour milk and molasses. If mixture is too stiff, thin with a little water. If raisins are used, either add to dry mixture before liquid or reserve enough flour to coat and add last. Fill well greased molds ⅔ full. Baking powder cans or other cans, with lids, may be used. Steam about 2 hours.

Mrs. David E. Galbraith

MOTHER'S BROWN BREAD

2 cups whole wheat flour	1 teaspoon soda
1 cup white flour	1 teaspoon baking powder
¾ cup brown sugar	1½ cups sour milk or buttermilk
1 cup raisins	1 teaspoon salt
1 tablespoon melted shortening	

(½ cup raisins and ½ cup nuts may be used instead of the 1 cup raisins.) Mix dry ingredients together. Add other ingredients. Use empty No. 2 cans with gold lining for baking cans. Put batter in three greased cans; fill ½ full. Let stand for 20 minutes. Bake 45 minutes in 350° oven.

Mrs. Arthur Stupka

HOE CAKE

*Workers in the cotton fields first
cooked this bread on their hoes
over little campfires. It is also
called "corn dodger."*

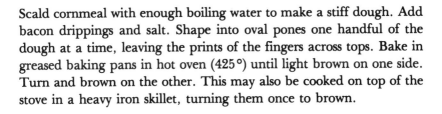

HOE CAKE

4 cups cornmeal
1 teaspoon salt
Boiling water
1 tablespoon bacon drippings

Scald cornmeal with enough boiling water to make a stiff dough. Add
bacon drippings and salt. Shape into oval pones one handful of the
dough at a time, leaving the prints of the fingers across tops. Bake in
greased baking pans in hot oven (425°) until light brown on one side.
Turn and brown on the other. This may also be cooked on top of the
stove in a heavy iron skillet, turning them once to brown.

Mrs. Henry W. Lix

TENNESSEE HOE CAKES

2 cups cornmeal
½ teaspoon salt
½ cup boiling water
½ cup cold water
Bacon fat or other shortening

Mix thoroughly. Shape with hands into oblong cakes. Bake on a well
greased griddle, turning when partly done so both sides will be brown.

Mrs. W.P. Trotter

HUSH PUPPIES

2 cups cornmeal
1 tablespoon flour
2 teaspoons baking powder
1 teaspoon salt

1 egg, beaten
2 cups milk
6 tablespoons chopped onion

Sift the dry ingredients into a bowl; mix egg with the milk and onion. Fold in the dry ingredients and beat until smooth. Drop by tablespoonfuls into a kettle of deep, hot fat. Cook until a light golden brown. Drain on a paper towel, and eat while hot.

Mrs. Dewey Ealy

HUSH PUPPIES

2 cups meal
1 onion, chopped fine
2 tablespoons flour

1 egg
3 teaspoons baking powder
1 teaspoon salt

Add enough of sweet milk to a mix a stiff batter. Spoon into deep pan with hot fat. Cook at 350° until done. Will make 24 puppies.

Mrs. W.P. Trotter

HUSH PUPPIES

Sift together:
¾ cup cornmeal
¼ cup flour
1 teaspoon baking powder
¼ teaspoon salt

Beat:
1 egg

Add:
6 tablespoons milk
2 tablespoons grated onion

Stir the liquids all at once into cornmeal mixture, and drop by spoonfuls into deep, hot (315°) fat or salad oil. Cook until golden brown. Makes about 12.

Mrs. Granville B. Liles

16

MY GRANDMOTHER'S CORN PONE

2 cups cornmeal
1 teaspoon salt

½ teaspoon soda
1 egg, beaten

Make a thickish mush of the cornmeal, salt and soda. Let it cook thoroughly. Stir in the egg, and drop small tablespoons onto hot baking pan with about ¼ inch bacon fat in it. Cook in a hot oven (450°). Baste once with hot fat. Crumbled bacon in the mixture is wonderful — at least it was wonderful when I ate it as a child. Serve right out of the pan, very hot.

Mrs. T.L. de Onativia

CORN PONE

1 quart cornmeal
½ teaspoon soda
1 egg

1 cup molasses
1 teaspoon salt

To one quart cornmeal add warm water, enough to make a thin dough. Place in warm place and let rise overnight. To this add molasses, soda, salt, and egg. Mix well and bake in a deep pan. Also good when cold to slice and fry.

This recipe has been used by the Dunn family for over one hundred years.

Mrs. Clifton Dunn

corn sheller

17

CORN STICKS

1 whole egg
   or
2 egg yolks

1 cup buttermilk
¾ cup cornmeal

2 tablespoons flour
½ teaspoon soda
½ teaspoon baking powder
½ teaspoon salt
2 tablespoons melted bacon fat
   or shortening

Beat egg. Add buttermilk and shortening. Sift flour and baking powder, soda, and salt. Add with meal to egg mixture. Have cornstick pans very hot. Grease. Pour in batter. Bake at 400° for about 10 minutes. Makes 2 pans corn sticks.

Mrs. Robert F. Gibbs

CORN STICKS

1½ cups water
½ cup molasses
1 teaspoon salt
1 cup cornmeal

¾ cup flour
2 teaspoons baking powder
3 tablespoons bacon drippings

Put water, molasses, and salt in a saucepan. Bring to a boil. Add the cornmeal. Cook until the mixture is stiff. When cool, add flour and baking powder sifted together. Form the mixture into sticks about 5 inches long and 1 inch thick. Put 1 cup of bacon drippings in a shallow baking pan. When fat is smoking, add corn sticks, shaking them so that each will be coated with the drippings. Then bake them in a hot oven about 18 minutes.

Mrs. W.P. Trotter

SPRING TONIC

My mother used to mix up molasses and sulphur to give for colds. She mixed 1 teaspoon molasses for each teaspoon sulphur. Give one teaspoonful to each child after mixing.

Mrs. Guy Cable

18

POT LIKKER DUMPLINGS

This originated in Tennessee, traveled to Alabama and Texas more than 100 years ago. My mother learned to make them from my grandmother.

You must have one large pot of turnip greens boiled with ham hocks. Start from scratch, with turnip greens fresh out of the patch and smoked hambone or ham hocks. Or use chopped turnip greens canned, simmered an hour with the ham, which should already be boiled tender. Mix 2 tablespoons minced onion (fresh, young ones with part of the green tops are best) into 1½ cups unsifted cornmeal. Season with ½ teaspoon salt and ¼ teaspoon black pepper. Stir in enough boiling pot liquor from the greens to make a stiff dough. When slightly cooled, mix in one egg thoroughly. Take this by spoonfuls and shape into small patties about ½ inch thick. Lay them gently on the top of the simmering greens. Cover and simmer 10 or 15 minutes or until done.

Mrs. Henry W. Lix

CORNMEAL DUMPLINGS

1 quart cornmeal   ½ teaspoon salt

Wet up with cold water until stiff. Make into little balls, put them in a kettle, pour boiling chicken or beef stock or pot liquor from greens or hambone over them, and boil for nearly an hour. Serve with meats.

Mrs. John O. Morrell

CORNMEAL DUMPLINGS

1 cup cornmeal
¼ teaspoon black pepper
Pinch of red pepper, if desired
Ham stock

Have ham stock boiling. Pour some over meal mixture and stir into dough stiff enough to drop from spoon, balls about the size of an egg. Drop in briskly boiling stock, then turn heat low. Simmer about 20 minutes.

Mrs. Dewey R. Ealy

CORNMEAL LIVER MUSH

My husband's mother made this kind of liver mush.

2 cups liver   ¾ cup fat

Cook liver well done. Have 1½ cups stock. Take ¾ cup cornmeal and parch cornmeal good and brown. Add stock and stir until good and thick. Then add liver and fat. Grind liver and fat. Add 1 teaspoon sage. Salt and pepper to taste.

Mrs. Ben C. Fisher

OLD TIME CORNMEAL MUSH

Cornmeal
One pint of water put in a quart cup
½ teaspoon salt

Bring water to a hot boil and take meal and just add a small amount at a time and stir all the time until the mush becomes thick. Remove from pan into dish. It is very good with cold sweet milk, or some like it sliced and fried in fat.

Mrs. Carlos T. Huskey

MUSH

Put one quart of water in a half-gallon kettle. Add 1 teaspoon of salt. Let come to a boil. Then stir in slowly about one cup of cornmeal. Cook slowly until it gets thick. Serve while hot with whole milk.

Mrs. Ennis Ownby

CORNMEAL CEREAL

1 or 1½ quarts boiling water
1 teaspoon salt
Cornmeal

Sprinkle enough cornmeal into boiling water to make a thickness like oatmeal, stirring all the time. When well done, serve with cream and sugar. The pioneers used molasses in place of sugar. This cornmeal cereal can be sliced when cold and fried in bacon fat and served with bacon.

Mrs. Ben C. Fisher

SCRAPPLE

Scrapple is a most palatable dish. Take out the heart and any lean scraps of pork, and boil until it will slip easily from the bones. Remove the fat, gristles and bones; then chop fine. Set aside the liquor in which the meat was boiled until cold. Take the cake of fat from the surface, and return to the fire. When it boils, put in the chopped meat, and season well with pepper and salt. Let it boil again. Then thicken with cornmeal as you would in making ordinary cornmeal mush. Cook one hour, stirring constantly at first, then putting back on the stove to boil gently. When done, pour in a long pan to mold. This can be kept several weeks in cold weather. Cut in slices and fry brown as you do mush. A delicious breakfast dish.

Mrs. W.P. Trotter

CORNBREAD CHICKEN STUFFING

The recipe for bread stuffing given is based on one quart of ½-inch crumbs cut or torn from sliced cornbread. For making it, cornbread that is a day old is better than fresh.

1 quart breadcrumbs
⅓ cup fat
¾ cup chopped celery
3 tablespoons chopped parsley
2 tablespoons chopped onion
½ to ¾ teaspoon salt
Pepper to taste

Melt fat in frying pan; add celery, parsley, and onion and cook a few minutes. Add to crumbs with the seasonings. Mix lightly but well. The dressed weight of the chicken should be 3 to 4 pounds. The oven temperature should be 350°, and time to bake 1½ to 2 hours.

Mrs. Guy Cable

CORNMEAL STUFFING

1 tablespoon meat drippings
   (bacon or chicken fat)
1½ cups cornmeal
4 cups water
1 cup chopped onion

1 tablespoon chopped parsley
1 teaspoon thyme
1 teaspoon sage
1 egg
Salt and pepper to taste

Heat drippings in frying pan. Add all remaining ingredients in order given. Cook, stirring to keep from burning, until dried down and well done before stuffing fowl.

Mrs. Henry W. Lix

CORNMEAL GRAVY with liver

¾ cup cornmeal
½ cup milk

1 cup water
Salt, pepper to taste

Salt and pepper liver and roll in cornmeal and fry in plenty of fat, having grease left over to make the gravy. Add the cornmeal to hot fat, letting brown well. Then add milk, water, salt and pepper. Cook until done. Serve with liver or any kind of fresh meats.

Mrs. Ben C. Fisher

CORNMEAL GRAVY

Fry about 4 or 5 good pieces of side meat. Have enough shortening in pan to cover cornmeal. Add about ½ cup of meal and 1 teaspoon of salt. Brown meal to a light brown. Then add 2½ cups of milk. Stir until it boils. Serve while hot.

Mrs. Ennis Ownby

CORNMEAL GRUEL

1½ cups water
⅓ teaspoon salt
1 slightly rounded tablespoon cornmeal

Have the water salted and actively boiling; shake the meal gently into it and cook 20 minutes, stirring constantly; then turn the whole into a double boiler and cook 2 hours. Strain if desired.

Mary Ruth Chiles

CORNMEAL PANCAKES

Used by my mother

2 teaspoons sugar
1 teaspoon salt
1 tablespoon baking powder
1¼ cups sifted flour

¾ cup cornmeal
2 eggs, well beaten
1¼ cups milk
3 tablespoons melted shortening

Sift together sugar, salt, baking powder, and flour. Stir in cornmeal. Combine eggs and milk and add to flour mixture. Add shortening and mix until smooth. Drop by tablespoonfuls onto lightly greased hot griddle. Cook until edges are brown and bubbles are in the middle. Turn and cook on other side. Serve butter and sorghum with pancakes.

Mrs. Arthur Stupka

spider - an iron
skillet on legs

CORNMEAL WAFFLES

1 cup cornmeal
1 cup flour
4 teaspoons baking powder
4 tablespoons sugar

½ teaspoon salt
Scant cup milk
2 well-beaten eggs
4 tablespoons melted fat

Mix and sift dry ingredients; add milk gradually; then eggs and melted fat. Drop a tablespoon on each section of waffle iron. Bake until crisp and brown.

Mary Ruth Chiles

CORNMEAL FLAPJACKS

This is how my husband makes cornmeal flapjacks. He uses this when he goes fishing and camping, to eat with his fish.

1 cup sour milk
1 cup water
½ cup flour

1 teaspoon soda
1 teaspoon salt

Stir in sifted cornmeal til thick. Then dip mixing spoonfuls into hot grease like pancakes. Brown on each side. Serve while hot with butter or use for bread with any food. Add an egg if you like. They are real good.

Mrs. Willard Nations

FRIED CORNBREAD

Good with black-eyed peas and greens.

1 cup cornmeal
Lard, size of walnut

½ teaspoon salt
1 teaspoon sugar

Mix ingredients and pour enough boiling water over to make batter. Fry as hot cakes.

Mrs. Dewey Ealy

MOLASSES AND BUTTER SPREAD

For hot biscuits and corn battercakes

1 cup molasses
⅓ cup soft butter

Molasses must be the thick, rich kind; either ribbon cane or sorghum may be used. Work molasses and butter together until mixture is creamy. Warm molasses slightly if they are too stiff before adding butter.

Mrs. Henry W. Lix

CORNMEAL MUFFINS

1 cup sifted flour
2 tablespoons sugar
2 eggs, well beaten
1 cup milk

2¼ teaspoons baking powder
1½ cups cornmeal
¾ teaspoon salt
4 tablespoons melted shortening

Sift flour once; measure; add baking powder, sugar, and salt, and sift again. Add cornmeal and mix well. Combine eggs, milk, and shortening; add to flour stirring only enough to dampen all flour. Bake in greased muffin pans in hot oven (425°) 25 minutes or until done. Makes 12 muffins.

Mrs. W.P. Trotter

CORNMEAL MUFFINS

4 tablespoons shortening
2 tablespoons sugar
1 egg
1¼ cups milk

1 cup flour
1 cup cornmeal
4 teaspoons baking powder
½ teaspoon salt

Cream shortening and sugar; add the well beaten eggs; then flour, baking powder, and salt sifted together and mix with cornmeal. Add milk gradually. Beat well. Bake in well greased muffin pans in hot oven (450°) about 25 minutes.

Mrs. W.P. Trotter

MOLASSES MUFFINS

2 cups sifted flour
3 teaspoons baking powder
3 tablespoons sugar
½ teaspoon salt
½ teaspoon ginger (or other spice)
1 egg, unbeaten
⅓ cup dark molasses
¾ cup milk

Put flour, baking powder, sugar, salt, and ginger into bowl. Drop shortening onto flour at one side. Add egg, molasses, and milk. Cut shortening into small pieces (size of pea) with fork or blender. Stir all contents until flour is moistened, ingredients just mixed. Batter will be lumpy. Fill muffin tins ⅔ full. Bake 15 to 20 minutes at 400°. Makes 8 large or 12 medium sized muffins.

Mrs. Fred A. Wingeier

HONEY MUFFINS

4 tablespoons melted shortening
2 tablespoons honey
1 egg
2 cups flour
4 teaspoons baking powder
½ teaspoon salt
¼ cup milk

Mix together shortening and honey. Add well beaten egg. Sift together dry ingredients. Add to first mixture alternately with milk. Beat well. Half fill greased muffin pans and bake in moderate oven (400°) about 25 minutes. Makes 12 muffins.

Mrs. W.P. Trotter

CORNMEAL CUSTARD PIE

3 eggs
1 cup milk
¾ cup cornmeal
1 teaspoon lemon flavoring

¾ cup sugar
2 tablespoons butter
2 pints boiling water

Make meringue of whites of 2 eggs. To the two pints of boiling water, sprinkle in the cornmeal, stirring constantly so it will not lump (if it seems too stiff you may add a little extra water). Cook for about 15 minutes, stirring constantly, until it is like a well-done mush. Add the butter, salt, and sugar, stirring well; then add the milk and flavoring. Set aside to cool, then add the well beaten eggs, stirring all the time. Pour into a pie pan lined with uncooked crust. Bake at once in hot oven.

Mrs. G.A. Powell

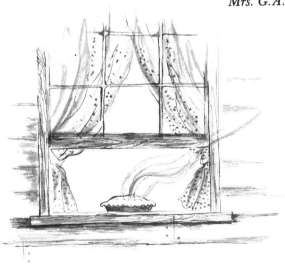

FOR INFANT'S COLDS

Roast an onion wrapped in a wet cloth on hot ashes until soft. Peeling the outside off and mashing them, apply on a cloth to the hollow of the child's feet.

Mrs. W.P. Trotter

OLD FASHIONED LEMON PIE

¼ pound butter
1 cup sugar
3 eggs, well beaten

2 teaspoons sifted cornmeal
Juice of one one lemon and
    grated rind

Cream butter and sugar. Mix cornmeal, juice and rind into butter and sugar mixture. Add beaten eggs. Bake 35 minutes in 350° oven.

Mrs. Dewey R. Ealy

CHESS PIE

5 eggs
1 cup milk
1 tablespoon flour

2 cups sugar
½ cup butter
1 tablespoon cornmeal

Beat egg yolks. Add sugar, then melted butter, flour and cornmeal. Beat well. Add milk. Put in uncooked pie crust. Bake in moderate oven (350°) for 45 minutes. Make meringue of egg white.

Mrs. Dewey R. Ealy

TAMALIE PIE

1 tablespoon lard
1 pound hamburger
1 large onion, cut fine
2 cups sifted cornmeal

Dash of chili powder
1 teaspoon salt
6 cups boiling water
1 pint tomatoes

Make cornmeal mush. Cook until fairly thick. Then put a layer of mush in a baking dish (about half the nush). In a separate pan put hamburger and onion in to brown. When well browned, add tomatoes, salt and chili powder. Let cook for 5 minutes; put in the dish with the cornmeal mush. Put the rest of the mush on top of the meat mixture. Lay 2 or 3 strips of bacon across top. Bake in hot oven 45 minutes. Serve with tomato catsup and crackers, pickles and olives.

Mrs. Dewey R. Ealy

BAKED CORNMEAL PUDDING

2 cups cornmeal
1 cup flour
2 well beaten eggs
¼ cup shortening
1 cup sorghum molasses

¼ teaspoon allspice
1 level teaspoon soda
1 level teaspoon salt
1 cup buttermilk

Sift meal twice. Thoroughly mix all dry ingredients. Add eggs, milk, molasses and shortening. Mix all together thoroughly, adding more milk if too stiff. Bake in well greased pudding pan until a golden brown. Test with toothpick; it comes out clean when pudding is done. Serve hot with any kind of fruit. It is delicious.

Mrs. J. T. Walker

*After reading **News and Views** and seeing so many requests for old timey recipes, I decided I'd send a few that were handed down to me from my mother and my grandmother. They, as myself, were born and reared right here in the foothills of dear Old Smoky.*

STEAMED SUET PUDDING

3 cups sifted flour
1 teaspoon soda
1 teaspoon cinnamon
1 teaspoon cloves
½ teaspoon grated nutmeg

1 teaspoon salt
1 cup suet
1 cup molasses
1 cup raisins

Mix and sift dry ingredients, keeping ½ cup flour to sift over raisins. Chop the suet fine and add it to the milk and molasses. Combine the two mixtures and add the raisins dredged with flour. Grease pudding molds or baking powder cans, and fill ⅔ full of the mixture. Cover and steam for 3 hours. Serve with hard sauce or any desired liquid sauce.

Hard Sauce: ⅓ cup butter
1 cup powdered sugar (or granulated
         sugar, brown sugar, or maple sugar)
1 teaspoon vanilla or other flavoring

Cream the butter until very soft, then stir in sugar and flavoring. Set in a cool place until required for use.

Mrs. Joe Kulesza

BLACK PUDDING

1 cup molasses
1 scant teaspoon soda
1 cup buttermilk
1 cup chopped suet
1 cup seedless raisins

½ cup blanched almonds
½ cup shredded citron
6 chopped figs
3 apples, chopped
3 cups flour

Mix well and place in greased and floured mold or bag and steam for three hours. Serve with hard sauce.

Mrs. John O. Morrell

CHRISTMAS PUDDING

3 cups flour
1 cup cornmeal
1½ cups sweet milk
1 cup raisins
1 cup currants
½ teaspoon soda

1½ cups suet, chopped fine
2 large tablespoons molasses
½ teaspoon cloves
½ teaspoon cinnamon
Pinch of salt

Add more milk if too stiff. Steam 3 hours.

Mrs. John O. Morrell

MOLASSES PUDDING

½ of a beaten egg
    or
1½ tablespoons beaten egg

1 tablespoon sugar
¼ cup molasses

1 tablespoon melted butter
¾ cup flour
½ teaspoon soda
¼ cup boiling water
¼ cup chopped black walnuts
¼ cup currants

Add sugar and molasses to beaten egg and beat well. Add melted butter. Add sifted flour, a little at a time; then the soda mixed with the boiling water. Add nut meats and currants. Place in greased pudding pan and cover with waxed paper or regular cover; or use 2 peanut cans with lids. Steam 2 hours. Makes 2 peanut can sized puddings.

Mary Ruth Chiles

PERSIMMON PUDDING

1 quart persimmons
1 good-sized raw sweet potato
1 pint rich milk
Butter, the size of an egg
2 eggs, well beaten
1 tablespoon sugar
Enough flour to make a medium
    stiff batter

Bake in slow oven until done. Serve with a sweet dip. Juicy persimmons are better than dry mealy ones since they are easier to remove seeds from. Persimmons are to be squeezed through coarse cheesecloth to remove seeds and skins. This is the way it used to be done.

Mrs. J. O. Morrell

PERSIMMON PUDDING

2 cups persimmon pulp
1 cup sugar
2 cups buttermilk
1 tablespoon melted butter
1 teaspoon soda

1 teaspoon baking powder
1 teaspoon cinnamon
¼ teaspoon salt
1½ cups flour
3 eggs, separated

Sieve the persimmons and add egg yolks. Beat well. Add sugar and beat again. Sift flour with salt, soda, baking powder, and cinnamon. Add to persimmon mixture alternately with the buttermilk. Fold in stiffly beaten egg whites; pour into greased 2-quart casserole and bake 40 to 50 minutes at 350°. Serve with whipped cream. This recipe can be halved for smaller families.

Mrs. Granville B. Liles

STACK CAKE

This recipe was used for many years by Mrs. Dolphus Kerley of Waynesville, North Carolina, who died January 6, 1948, two months before reaching 90 years of age. This recipe was used by her mother, Mrs. Drury Bigham, of the Allens Creek section of Haywood County, North Carolina.

¾ cup shortening
1 cup sugar
1 cup sorghum molasses
3 eggs
1 cup milk

4 cups wheat flour
2 teaspoons baking powder
½ teaspoon soda
1 teaspoon salt

Sift well flour, salt, soda, and baking powder. Cream shortening, then add sugar a little at a time, blending well. Add sorghum and mix thoroughly. Add eggs one at a time, beating well until smooth. Pour ⅓-inch deep in greased 9-inch pans and bake. This will make 6 or 7 layers. When cool, stack layers using about 3 cups of sweetened, slightly spiced applesauce.

Mrs. Louise Liner

MOLASSES FRUIT CAKE

(Old-fashioned Stack Cake)

½ cup sour milk or buttermilk
Spice to taste (allspice or nutmeg)
½ cup shortening
½ teaspoon soda
1 cup molasses
1 egg

Mix ingredients well. Then add enough flour to make a stiff dough. Roll thin and cut layers round, the size of cake desired, and bake. To stack use approximately 1 quart cooked dried apples or canned apples; drain juice, mash, and sweeten to taste. Use between layers.

Mrs. Clifton Dunn

NAOMI'S OLD FASHIONED STACK CAKE

½ cup shortening
½ cup sugar
⅓ cup molasses
1 egg, well beaten
½ cup buttermilk
3½ cups flour

2 teaspoons baking powder
½ teaspoon soda
½ teaspoon salt
1 teaspoon ginger
1 teaspoon vanilla

Cream sugar and shortening together. Add the egg, molasses, buttermilk, and mix well. Sift flour, baking powder, salt, soda, and ginger together, and add to the other mixture. Mix well. Add vanilla. It makes a dough. Roll out as for a pastry; cut to fit a 9-inch cake pan or heavy skillet. Bake at 350° for 10 to 12 minutes. When cool, stack the layers with highly spiced and sweetened applesauce, or better still, with old-fashioned dried apples, cooked, sweetened, and spiced.

Mrs. John Rogers

APPLE STACK PIE

½ cup shortening
1 cup sugar
2 eggs
½ cup molasses
1 teaspoon baking powder

1 teaspoon soda
¼ teaspoon salt
½ cup milk
5 cups flour

Cream shortening and sugar. Add eggs, molasses, and milk. Sift flour, baking powder, soda, salt. Work flour in until stiff. Roll out in a thin layer. Cut out size of a plate. Makes 6 layers. Bake in oven at 350° for 10 minutes a layer. Put fruit between layers.

If you use dried fruit, 1 pint before it is cooked; cook and add 1 teaspoon of cinnamon. Or 3 cups of cooked apples and 1 teaspoon of cinnamon.

Mrs. Verlis Ownby

"sad iron"

UPSIDE DOWN APPLE GINGERBREAD

An OLD family favorite

2 tablespoons butter	1 teaspoon cinnamon
1 cup brown sugar	3 or 4 tart apples, sliced thin

Melt the butter in a heavy baking pan. Sprinkle the brown sugar and cinnamon over the butter. Arrange the apples in the pan in overlapping layers. Pour over it the following batter:

¼ cup shortening	1¼ cups flour
¼ cup brown sugar	¼ teaspoon salt
1 beaten egg	¾ teaspoon ginger
½ cup molasses	½ teaspoon cinnamon
½ cup boiling water, butter-milk, or sour milk	¾ teaspoon soda

Cream shortening until soft. Gradually add the sugar and continue creaming until smooth. Add the egg and molasses and beat light. Add the water or milk alternately with the flour, which has been sifted with the salt, spices, and soda, mixing thoroughly after each addition. Bake in moderate oven (350°) 30 to 40 minutes. Serve warm with either hard sauce or whipped cream. Serves 6 to 8.

Mrs. David E. Galbraith

SPONGE GINGERBREAD

1 cup molasses
½ cup sugar
½ cup butter
1 teaspoon ginger
2 teaspoons soda dissolved in 1 cup boiling water

1 teaspoon cloves
1 teaspoon cinnamon
2½ cups flour
2 eggs

Cream butter and sugar; add eggs; beat well. Add molasses. Add the dry ingredients, sifted, alternately with the hot water. Pour into greased and floured pan and bake about 40 minutes at 350°.

Mrs. G.B. Liles

GINGER CAKE

This recipe is over 150 years old.

1 cup sugar
1 cup shortening
1 cup molasses
1 cup boiling water
2 eggs, well beaten

3 cups flour
1 teaspoon cloves
½ teaspoon ginger
1 teaspoon cinnamon

Cream shortening; add sugar, then molasses, finally all the boiling water. Add sifted dry ingredients, stirring well after each addition. Finally add the well beaten eggs. Bake at 350° for 30 to 35 minutes.

Mrs. Reaford McCarter

GINGERBREAD

½ cup butter
1 cup sugar
1 egg
1 cup molasses

1 cup sour milk
1 teaspoon soda
1 teaspoon ginger
3 cups flour

Cream butter; add sugar, well beaten egg, molasses, then the sour milk to which soda has been added. Sift flour and ginger together. Add flour and mix well. Pour into greased pan and bake in a moderate oven.

Mrs. Roy Pilkington

bees making
sourwood honey

HONEY CRISPS

3 cups flour
¾ cup shortening
1 egg

1 teaspoon salt
½ cup sugar
½ cup honey
1 tablespoon orange juice
½ teaspoon vanilla
½ teaspoon orange extract

Sift together flour and salt. Cream together shortening and sugar. Add egg, beating well. Add honey, orange juice, vanilla, and orange extract, blending well. Stir in flour mixture. Chill dough. Roll out about 1/8 inch thick on lightly floured board. Cut out with floured cookie cutter. Bake on greased baking sheet in moderate oven (350°) about 8 minutes. Yield about 9 dozen cookies.

Mrs. W. P. Trotter

HONEY CINNAMON TOAST

Cut thin slices of whole wheat bread. Toast on both sides until well browned. Spread the toast with butter and with a paste made of honey and cinnamon mixed according to taste. Serve hot.

Mrs. W.P. Trotter

"bee gums"

HONEY CAKE

½ cup shortening
1 cup honey
1 egg, well beaten
½ cup sour milk

1 teaspoon baking powder
2 cups flour
½ teaspoon cinnamon

Cream shortening. Add honey and egg. Sift flour; measure and sift with baking powder, salt, and cinnamon. Add milk alternately with dry mixture. Mix thoroughly. Pour into shallow, well-oiled pan. Bake in moderate oven (375°) 50 minutes.

Mrs. W.P. Trotter

HONEY WAFERS

1 cup butter
1 cup sugar
4 cups flour

2 cups strained honey
2 teaspoons lemon extract
1 teaspoon salt

Mix well and spread on greased cookie sheet about 1/8 inch deep. Bake at 350°. When done cut into squares and roll on handle of wooden spoon while still warm. Dust with confectioners sugar and store to ripen.

Mrs. John O. Morrell

PUMPKIN CHIPS

Cut peeled pumpkin strips into chips about the thickness of a dollar. To every pound of chips add a pound of sugar and the juice of one lemon. Let stand overnight. By morning there will be juice sufficient to cook it in. Cut lemon rinds into strips and boil until tender. Add to pumpkin and boil until pumpkin chips look clear. Cook on slow fire.

Mrs. John O. Morrell

DRIED APPLE FRUIT CAKE

Soak 3 cups of dried apples overnight in cold water enough to swell them. Chop them in the morning. Put them on the fire with 2 cups of molasses. Stir until soft. Add 1½ cups seedless raisins. Stew a few moments. When cold add:

3½ cups flour	2 eggs
1 cup butter	1 teaspoon soda dissolved in
2 cups sugar	1 cup sweet milk
beaten to a cream	

Beat thoroughly. This will make 2 good-sized cakes. The apples will cook like citron and taste delicious. Bake in a steady oven. Spices may be added. This is not a dear but a delicious cake.

Mrs. W.P. Trotter

drying apples in the sun

CORNMEAL COOKIES

1 cup shortening
1½ cups sugar
2 eggs
1 teaspoon lemon extract
½ cup seedless raisins

3 cups flour
1 cup cornmeal
1 teaspoon baking powder
1 teaspoon nutmeg
½ teaspoon salt

Cream shortening. Add sugar slowly. Beat well. Add eggs and beat thoroughly. Then add lemon extract. Dredge chopped raisins with ¼ cup flour and add. Mix and sift remaining flour with cornmeal and other dry ingredients and add. Roll on floured board and cut. Bake at 400° for 10 minutes.

Mrs. John O. Morrell

MOLASSES CRISPS

1¼ cups flour
¾ teaspoon soda
½ teaspoon ginger

½ cup molasses
¼ cup shortening

Sift the dry ingredients. In a sauce pan bring molasses and shortening to a boil. Cool slightly. Add flour mixture. Mix well. Chill thoroughly. Cut in desired shapes. Arrange on greased cookie sheet. At 375°, bake until done, about 8 to 10 minutes. Makes about 2 dozen.

Mrs. W.P. Trotter

HONEY COOKIES

⅔ cup shortening
½ cup sugar
1 cup strained honey
1 egg
5 cups flour
½ cup sour milk or cream

1 teaspoon soda
½ teaspoon cinnamon
½ teaspoon nutmeg
½ teaspoon cloves
½ teaspoon salt

Cream shortening and sugar; add honey and mix well. Beat egg and add to milk. Sift dry ingredients together and add alternately with milk. Chill. Roll out about ¼ inch thick; cut as desired, and bake at 350°. Makes about 4 dozen.

Mrs. J.O. Morrell

MOLASSES CANDY

Here is a recipe for old-time molasses candy. My grandmother Dunn said when she was growing up that folks had to grow everything they had to eat. Also had old-fashioned looms to weave cloth to make all their clothing, and at Christmas they had to make molasses candy. I have tried it myself and it is delicious.

Take 2 quarts of molasses. Put it in a large vessel (it boils over easily). Boil and stir it constantly to keep it from scorching (use medium heat). Cook until it will form a soft ball when you drop from a spoonful in real cold water. Now remove it from the heat. Let cool enough so you can handle it with your hands. Have a dish of butter or margarine handy. Grease your hands so the candy won't stick to your hands. Now take enough of the candy in your hands to make 2 or 3 sticks. Now pull the candy, double back and pull again. Keep pulling and working the candy. In about 5 minutes, the candy will turn light yellow in color. Then it is ready to cut in stick lengths. Stick it out to about the size of an ordinary stick of candy. Cut in stick lengths with a sharp knife. Wrap in waxed paper. Store in a cool place.

Mrs. J. T. Walker

sorghum making - boiling the syrup

MOLASSES CANDY

2 cups molasses
1 cup sugar

1 tablespoon vinegar
Butter, size of a walnut

Boil briskly and constantly for 20 minutes, stirring all the time. When cool enough, pull it quickly until it is white.

Mrs. J. O. Morrell

POPCORN BALLS

We make these in our Cub Scout Pack.

4 quarts popped corn
1 cup molasses
1 cup sugar
1 teaspoon vinegar

2 tablespoons butter
Few grains baking soda
½ teaspoon vanilla

Stir molasses, sugar, and vinegar together. Boil slowly. When a drop forms a hard ball in cold water, add butter and vanilla. Pour mixture into a bowl of popped corn and stir fast. When nearly cool, butter your hands, and roll popcorn into balls.

Jimmy Galbraith

HONEY TAFFY

1 cup strained honey
1 cup sugar

1 tablespoon butter
Few grains salt

Boil honey, salt, and sugar to hard ball stage, at 265-270°. Add butter. Pour into well buttered pan. Cool. Pull until white and porous. Cut into one-inch pieces.

Mrs. W.P. Trotter

HONEY SALAD DRESSING

¼ teaspoon dry mustard
½ teaspoon paprika
½ teaspoon salt

¾ cup salad oil
¼ cup honey
¼ cup vinegar or lemon juice

Combine dry ingredients. Blend in honey and add vinegar slowly.
Add oil slowly and beat well. Shake well just before serving.

Mrs. J. O. Morrell

HOT CIDER TODDY

⅔ cup strained honey
7 cups cider
1 apple
Whole cloves

1 orange
1 teaspoon grated orange rind
2 cups orange juice

Mix honey and 1 cup of cider well. Add rest of cider. Stud the apple
and orange with cloves. Add to cider and heat. Add rind and juice,
and heat for about 2 minutes longer. Serve piping hot.

Mrs. J. O. Morrell

cider press

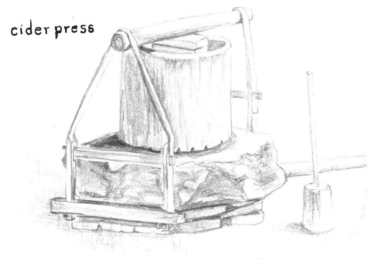

WHOOPING COUGH SYRUP

Used by my mother when we children had the whooping cough or bad colds. Is really good for whooping cough; very reliable cough mixture.

½ pound flax seed
1 cup granulated sugar
6 lemons (juice)
½ pound honey

Put flax seed in a bag; pour over it 1½ pints of water. Let simmer down to ½ that amount. Remove from fire and add other ingredients while still hot.

Dose: Give any amount as often as needed.

Half of recipe makes 1 pint.

Mrs. Stanley Cooley

46

FRIED TROUT

First, catch the fish!

Then clean it; leave the head on (this is optional). Put cornmeal in a paper sack with salt and pepper. Put the fish in the sack, and shake it up and down, to cover with cornmeal. Take a good-sized iron frying pan, and lay strips of bacon across the bottom of the pan. Then lay a layer of fish crosswise across the strips of bacon. Fry. When the bottom side is golden brown, take a tin plate and lay it on top of the fish in the frying pan. Turn the frying pan upside down and pour all the grease off. The fish will be lying on top of the tin plate. Start all over again by laying more strips of bacon on the bottom of the frying pan. Lay the fish on it, and cook until brown on the other side. When done, you will have a bunch of fish tied together with the bacon. They have been basted together. This is a particularly good way to cook small fish not over 10 inches in length.

Carlock E. Johnson

47

TROUT

Scrape off the scales of the rainbow beginning at the tail and scrape toward the head. The speckled trout doesn't have scales. Slit the fish on the bottom side and take out the intestines. Wash well. Salt and roll in sifted cornmeal. Fry in grease. Turn only once. When golden brown remove from the grease.

Mrs. Willard Nations

GROUND HOG

This is a recipe that my mother-in-law taught me how to cook ground hog.

Dress and cut it up. Put in pot, then bring to boil. Break up spicewood branches, and put in pot with meat. Boil until meat is tender. Remove; then salt and pepper; then roll in flour; put in ½ cup shortening, preferably bacon grease. Then put in oven and bake until it is brown.

Mrs. Ennis Ownby

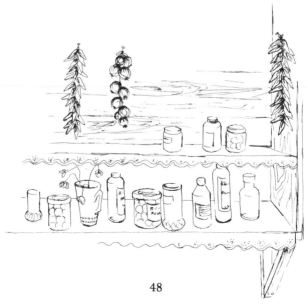

HOMINY

This is the way my mother made it.

Lye: Take a wooden box that will hold about half a bushel. Make a small hole in one end. Place end lower than the other that has the hole in it. Fill with hardwood ashes. Take a stone or glass jar, tie a white cloth over the top of the jar, and place under the hole in the box. Then pour water on the ashes until the lye starts coming out of the hole.

My grandmother had an ash hopper made for the purpose of dripping lye to make hominy.

Hominy: Now shell 3 or 4 ears of corn, white or yellow. Put the corn in an iron pot; cover the corn with the lye you have dripped out of the ashes. Cook until the eyes and outer skin come off the corn. Keep covered with lye all the time. When the outer skin and eyes look like they are all off, pour into a pan and rinse and rub until all the eyes and skin are off, changing water often. Then put in a clean pot, cover with water, and salt to taste. Cook until tender. You can eat it this way or fry in grease. It's just fine.

Mrs. Willard Nations

CURE FOR RINGWORM

Yellow dock root or leaves steeped in vinegar will cure the worst case of ringworm.

Mrs. W.P. Trotter

TOMATO FRITTERS

2 cups tomatoes
1 cup cornmeal
½ teaspoon salt

Mix dry ingredients into tomatoes and fry brown in a hot pan of grease. Makes 8 fritters.

Mrs. Guy Cable

CORNMEAL FOR CRUMBS

For a change, use waterground cornmeal instead of bread or cracker crumbs in which to roll croquettes, fish, or oysters before frying in deep fat or sauteeing.

Mrs. H. W. Lix

FRIED OKRA

Tumble 4 cups okra cut crosswise, fresh or frozen and slightly thawed, in a bowl with 1 cup cornmeal. Season with 1 teaspoon salt and ¼ teaspoon black pepper. Saute in a heavy skillet with 4 tablespoons bacon drippings. This cooks in about 10 or 15 minutes. Use medium flame. Green tomatoes are also delicious cooked this way.

Mrs. Henry W. Lix

SAUERKRAUT

Trim off outer leaves of white cabbage and wash heads thoroughly in cold salted water. Shave it fine on a cabbage cutter, rejecting the tough stalks or reserving them to pickle along with the cabbage.

old fashioned
Kraut cutter

To each peck of cabbage allow a pint of fine salt. Wash the outer green leaves of the cabbage in cold salted water, and use them to line a wooden tub. Put the cabbage in the tub with layers of the salt, beating all of it until it is tightly packed down. Put a board over the cabbage with a heavy stone on it.

Let it stand for at least six weeks, when it will be ready to use.

Mrs. John O. Morrell

BAKED BEANS

2½ cups dry beans	1¼ teaspoons salt
¼ cup sorghum	¾ teaspoon dry mustard
½ cup catsup	Sliced onions
½ pound salt pork or bacon	Brown sugar

Sort beans and run clear water over them in a colander. Put in large pan and cover them with water three times the depth of beans. Let stand overnight. In the morning cook beans till tender. Put a few beans on a teaspoon and blow on them; skins will crack open when beans are tender. Drain beans and save liquid. Put beans in casserole or bean pot. Bury cubed pork in beans. Mix sorghum, catsup, salt, and mustard together. Pour over beans. Slice onions just to cover top of casserole. Put a small amount of brown sugar on each onion slice. Add bean liquid to reach top of beans. Cover casserole and bake 6 to 8 hours in 300° oven. Do not allow beans to cook dry. Add more liquid or water. Uncover last half hour if not brown.

Mrs. Arthur Stupka

FRIED APPLES

Place a piece of cow butter the size of a goose egg in a skillet. Add ½ cup of water, ½ cup of sorghum molasses. Fill pan with apples that have been quartered but not peeled. Cook slowly with lid on until apples are tender. Good with pork.

Mrs. Louise Liner

MOLASSES APPLE BUTTER

This kind of butter can be made with sweet potatoes or pumpkins in place of the apples.

      2 cups apples which have been cooked
      1 cup molasses
      Spices or flavoring if desired

Cook well, stirring all the time, until thick and buttery-like.

Mrs. Ben C. Fisher

"piggin"

BLACKBERRY JAM

Wash berries, any amount. Put in large kettle and heat slowly, stirring often until some of the juice cooks out. Cook berries until soft. Measure cooked berries and juice. Add ⅔ as much sugar as measured berries. Cook sugar and fruit rapidly, stirring occasionally and skimming foam from edge. Cook until thick. Juice will chop off short when dropped from a spoon; if juice sheets from spoon, jam will be too stiff. Can jam in half-pint ot pint sterilized jars. Ten cups of cooked fruit makes 4½ pints of jam.

Mrs. Arthur Stupka

WILD PLUM JAM

Use red wild plums. Wash plums and remove spots but do not remove seeds, as sweetest part is attached to seed. Put plums in pan with several tablespoons of water. Cook slowly until soft. Measure fruit; add an equal amount of sugar. Cook fruit and sugar until juice drops short from spoon; if juice sheets from spoon, jam will be too stiff. Can in sterilized half-pint or pint jars.

Mrs. Arthur Stupka

54